Life Lessons and

Reflections

Also by Montel Williams

Mountain, Get Out of My Way!

Practical Parenting
(co-authored with Jeffrey Gardère, Ph.D.)

Life Lessons
and Reflections

Montel Williams

MOUNTAIN
MOVERS
PRESS

An imprint of Hay House, Inc.
Carlsbad, California • Sydney, Australia

Published and distributed in the United States by:

Mountain Movers Press, an imprint of Hay House, Inc., P.O. Box 5100,
Carlsbad, CA 92018-5100 • (800) 654-5126 • (800) 650-5115 (fax)
Please visit the Hay House Website at: hayhouse.com

Editorial: Jill Kramer • Design: Christy Salinas
Cover photo and photo used on page 72: James Sorensen for Paramount
Photo on page 2: Williams family photo • All other interior photos: Jay Lee

Library of Congress Cataloging-in-Publication Data

Williams, Montel.
   Life lessons and reflections / Montel Williams.
      p.   cm.
   ISBN 1-58825-001-6 (hardcover)
   1. Multiple sclerosis--Patients--Conduct of life.   2. Conduct of life--Quotations,
   maxims, etc.   I. Title.

   RC377 .W556 2000
   082--dc21

                                                              00-056845

                          ISBN 1-58825-001-6

            03   02   01   00   4   3   2   1
                  1st printing, September 2000

         Printed in the United States of America by Palace Press

Contents

If ye have faith as a grain of mustard seed, ye shall say unto this mountain, Remove hence to yonder place; and it shall remove; and nothing shall be impossible unto you.

— Matthew 17:20

Mountain, get out
of my way!

— Montel Williams

Preface

Imagine what it would be like to one day wake up paralyzed or blind without any kind of warning. Imagine a nine-year-old girl who cannot attend school and has no friends because she has seizures that have permanently damaged her brain. These are actual cases of people with an insidious disease called multiple sclerosis (MS). MS strikes without warning and is often debilitating. It does not discriminate by age, gender, or race. (A recent survey conducted by Zogby International in June 2000 states that an alarming 2.8 million Americans suffer from multiple sclerosis.)

In honor of all the people dealing with this disease, I have pledged 100 percent of my author royalties from <u>Life Lessons and Reflections</u> to the fight against multiple sclerosis. (The organizations mentioned in this Preface will each receive grants from the Montel Williams MS Foundation to further their research in the hope of finding a cure.

My first reaction when I was diagnosed with MS was denial. I have a friend at Harvard named Dr. S. Allen Counter who is a prominent neuroscientist. I asked that he put me in touch with the best doctors in the field of neurology for a second opinion. He referred me to Drs. Michael Olek and Howard Weiner of Harvard, and Brigham and Women's Hospital in Boston. I became acquainted with The Foundation for Neurologic Diseases and the important work they are doing in providing treatment to MS patients. The Foundation supports clinical and basic research on multiple sclerosis. With Foundation funding, a new MS center at Brigham and Women's Hospital at Massachusetts General Hospital (BWH/MGH) opened in the spring of 2000. The BWH/MGH center (under Dr. Weiner's direction) is the only one in the country that offers comprehensive care for

MS patients. It has its own immunology lab, MRI magnet and clinical trials, as well as physical and occupational therapy and patient education. Using the most state-of-the art science and technology, the center aims to help people with MS live their lives as fully as possible.

Shortly after I announced my MS diagnosis, I had the good fortune to meet Nancy Davis. Our lives parallel each other in so many ways, and we became instant friends. Nancy also suffers from multiple sclerosis, and when her doctors told her to go home and lie in bed for the rest of her life, it was her call to action.

The Nancy Davis Center Without Walls is a unique collaboration of leading scientists at top hospitals and universities who are dedicated to erasing MS. The Nancy Davis Center brings together many researchers and clinicians throughout the country who are researching the disease, and it provides them with the opportunity to meet, talk, share discoveries, and advance the fight much faster than any one research unit could do alone. The Nancy Davis Center's theme is simple: communication—doctors working together toward a mutual goal. When this goal is reached, all will share in the victory.

In addition to the regular use of high-technology communication tools, researchers at The Nancy Davis Center come together to share scientific accomplishments through monthly telephone conference calls, scientific advisory meetings, and MS symposiums held four times a year in Los Angeles.

The Nancy Davis Center constantly strives to strengthen this revolutionary concept with new approaches to finding the best and the brightest minds in the field. Proposals and grants, submitted in standard National Institutes of Health (NIH) format, are reviewed by the Center's Scientific Advisory Board, spearheaded by Dr. George Eisenbarth at the University of Colorado Health Sciences Center.

The Nancy Davis Foundation holds an annual fundraising event to support the work of the Center Without Walls. I was honored to be named "The Man of Courage" at the 8th Annual Race to Erase MS event held in 2000. A grand total of two and a half million dollars was raised in that evening alone for the fight against MS.

Dr. S. Allen Counter also introduced me to the phenomenal doctors at The Karolinska Nobel Institute in Stockholm, Sweden. These physicians are at the forefront of groundbreaking research on MS, and I travel to the institute regularly for treatment and checkups.

Dr. Thomas Olsson, professor of Molecular Medicine, who leads the team of MS researchers at the Institute, has conducted studies on several forms of treatment of MS, including new medicines not presently on the market. Dr. Olsson's Molecular Medicine department is presently conducting Phase II trials with new medicines for the control and possible cure of MS. This department is allied with several ancillary ones at the Karolinska Institute that conduct studies on new ways to image MS lesions. For example, several labs allied with the Molecular Medicine and the Neuroradiology departments have advanced MRI techniques that can identify lesions or sites of inflammation that are difficult to image by conventional means.

Together, we can win this battle. We must persevere and never give up hope for finding a cure!

The Montel Williams MS Foundation
331 West 57th Street, Suite 420
New York, NY 10019

Introduction

Shakespeare said:

> "Sweet are the uses of adversity,
> which, like the toad,
> ugly and venomous, wears yet a
> precious jewel in his head."

This is what my diagnosis of multiple sclerosis (MS) has come to mean to me. It wasn't always this way. It took more than six months of denial before I was finally able to face the disease . . . then came the fear . . . then the anger. I've been known to say many times during the last year or so—since my battle with the disease has become more and more public:

"MS picked the wrong person.
I have a big mouth,
and I'm going to continue flapping
it until there's a cure!"

This blessing in disguise has taught me more about myself than I ever thought possible. I have also been humbled by the overwhelming outpouring of love and support from fans and fellow MS sufferers.

The following pages contain words that have inspired me in my life, and a few of my own words that, I've been told, have inspired others. Please savor them for the beauty that lies in each meaning.

Inspirational

Quotes

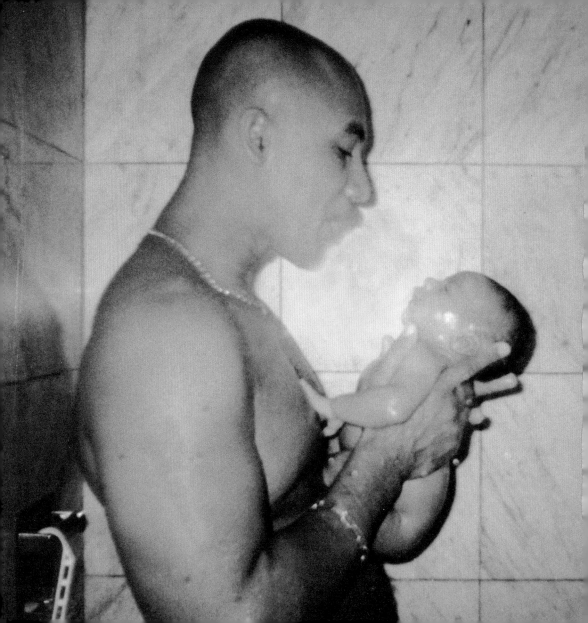

I am your
legacy.

You are my
future.

Together we can
move mountains.

Don't wait for your
ship to come in.
Swim out to it.

There are no secrets
to success. It's the
result of preparation,
hard work, learning
from failure.

— Colin Powell

One isn't necessarily born with courage, but one is born with potential. Without courage, we cannot practice any other virtue with consistency. We can't be kind, true, merciful, generous or honest.

— Maya Angelou

Love is the only force capable of transforming an enemy into a friend.

— Martin Luther King, Jr.

What shall it profit a man, if he shall gain the whole world, and lose his soul?

—Mark 8:36

Respect, by the book, suggests concern, thoughtfulness, the quality or state of being esteemed, or held in high regard. That's fine, but to me it also means trust, honesty, the ability to keep an open mind, and interacting with others without rancor or disdain.

It starts with ourselves, learning what trust is. And once we learn what trust is, then maybe we can share it with somebody else, and we'll make the world a better place to live.

Love truth, but pardon error.

—Voltaire

I don't think it is enough to simply applaud your kids and root for them to do well. It's plenty, and it's a start, but you also have to teach them to root for themselves, to know that they can do whatever they want, and that true valida-tion comes from within.

Life is either a daring adventure or nothing.
To keep our faces toward change and behave
like free spirits in the presence of fate is
strength undefeatable.

— Helen Keller

No violence! Make sure the words that come
out of your mouth are words that make your
children feel good about themselves-not words
that break their hearts.

Beauty is how you feel inside, and it reflects
in your eyes. It is not something physical.

—Sophia Loren

Restraint: look it up if you don't know what it means. For my purposes, it means stopping yourself from doing or saying something that might come back to hurt you or someone else. It is exercising control or moderation. It is pulling back when your impulse is to push forward. It doesn't mean you can't act with your heart, but you have to make sure your head is in the right place.

When pride comes,

then comes

disgrace, but with

humility comes

wisdom.

—Proverbs 11:2

The good thing about life is that you can learn from everything that happens. Today you may get an answer that will make you look inside yourself and make you see another piece of you. This may be what you needed so you can say, "I don't need to hold on to the past; I can just look to the future."

What did I do today that is worth talking about tomorrow?

Of all the passions, fear weakens judgement most.

—Cardinal de Ritz

The love that you
are looking for
is really the love inside
yourself.

I am a great believer in luck, the harder I
work, the more I have of it.

— Thomas Jefferson

To spare oneself from grief at all cost
can be achieved only at the price of total
detachment, which excludes the ability to
experience happiness.

— Erich Fromm

The thoughts we think and the words we
speak create our experiences.

— Louise Hay

Do not say things.
What you are
stands over you
the while and
thunders so that
I cannot hear
what you say to
the contrary.

— Emerson

Children need to be taught values. They need to be taught that there is a future for them, that there is some point in their lives where they can be helpful to others.

One can never consent to creep when one feels an impulse to soar.

— Helen Keller

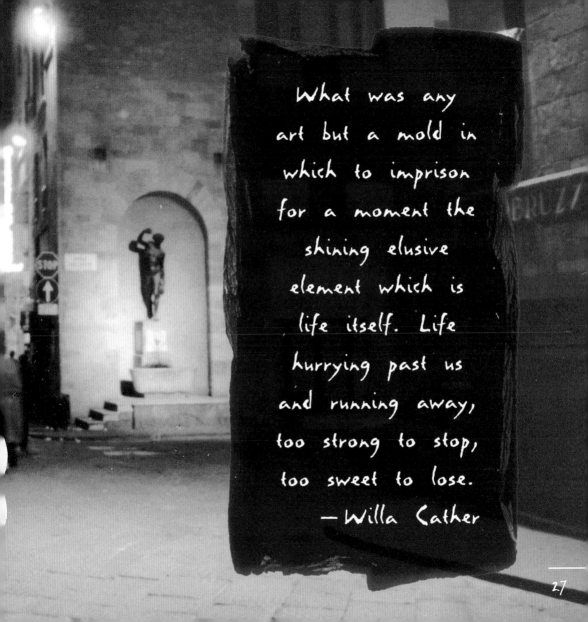

What was any
art but a mold in
which to imprison
for a moment the
shining elusive
element which is
life itself. Life
hurrying past us
and running away,
too strong to stop,
too sweet to lose.
— Willa Cather

There are no shortcuts in this world and no handouts. We've all got the same shot at the brass ring.

No one can make you feel inferior without your consent.

— Eleanor Roosevelt

Whoever is happy will make others happy too. He who has courage and faith will never perish in misery.

— Anne Frank

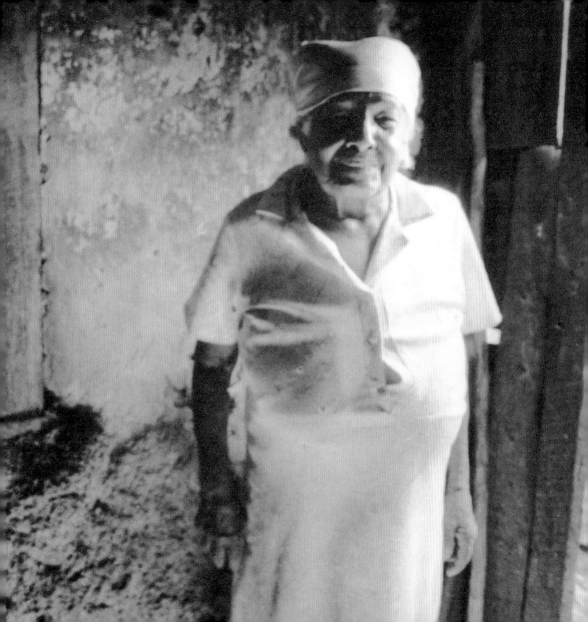

Unless you try to do something beyond what you have already mastered, you will never grow.

Some men see things as they are and ask why. Others dream things that never were and ask why not.

— George Bernard Shaw

Great spirits have often encountered violent opposition from weak minds.

— Albert Einstein

What counts is that we make an effort to step outside of ourselves and put someone else's needs ahead of our own.

We can't sweep things under the rug. We keep trying to walk around the stuff, or we keep tripping over it. The only way to solve a problem is to first pull back the rug and then deal with what's under there.

The seat of my pants invariably took me where I had to go.

Innovation

The best way to predict
the future is to create it.

The heart to conceive,
the understanding to
direct, and the hand to
execute.

— Anonymous

The first problem for all of us is not to learn but to unlearn.

— Gloria Steinem

However self sufficient we are, our strength is always being supplied by others unknown to us whose paths led them to our house at the moment we needed the light they could give.

— Howard Thurman

Man's inhumanity to man makes countless thousands mourn.

— Robert Burns

A friend of mine posted signs around his house to remind himself and his family that it was okay to disagree with each other—as long as they were considerate about it. That friend was Caldwell Williams, a successful motivational speaker who put his ideas into practice. His motto was: "Speak without offending, listen without defending."

Character builds slowly, but it can be torn down again with incredible swiftness.

— Faith Baldwin

Children will never learn responsibility if they can't recognize it in their parents.

When you cease to make a contribution you begin to die.

— Eleanor Roosevelt

There are mystically in our faces certain characteristics which carry in them the motto of our souls, wherein he that cannot read A, B, C may read our natures.

— Sir Thomas Browne

Do not regret growing older, it's a privilege denied to many.

— Anonymous

We stand on the brink of a precipice. We peer into the abyss—we grow sick and dizzy. Our first impulse is to shrink from the danger. Unaccountably we remain.

— Edgar Allan Poe

I am not afraid of storms, for I am learning how to sail my ship.

— Louisa May Alcott

A man's behavior is the index of the man, and his discourse is the index of his understanding.

— Ali Ibn-Ab-Talib

The most important thing in life is belonging.

Sometimes success is just a matter of hanging on.

Discipline builds character, character propels you toward your goals.

— Gemma Simmons

I believe wholeheartedly that if you complain about the ills of a society, then you do everything you can possibly do to change what you complain about.

They wrote documents hundreds of years ago stating that all men are created equal. We talk a mean game in this country, but we play a meaner one.

When my time is up and I stand before my maker, I'd like to be able to say, "God, I don't have one ounce of talent, love, compassion, or energy left. I used every gift you gave me."

You should be okay
with your image.
Don't let society
define you; define
yourself.

If children gave up
when they fell the
first time, they
would never learn
to walk.

— Louise Hay

Your character is the result of your conduct.

— Aristotle

I am afraid that what Albert Einstein said is true, "The tragedy of man is what dies inside a person as he lives."

Making a mistake doesn't mean it's all over. It doesn't mean you quit and live off that as an excuse for not being successful. You use that mistake as a springboard to becoming successful.

A living is defined by what you get. A life
is defined by what you give.

A pupil from whom nothing is ever demanded
which he cannot do, never does all he can.
—John Stuart Mill

The beauty of a man's soul shines out when a man bears with composure one heavy misfortune after another, not because he does not feel them, but because he is a man of higher heroic temper.

— Aristotle

Intentions often melt in the face of unexpected opportunity.

— Shirley Temple Black

That which does not kill me makes me
stronger.

— Nietzsche

Stories of Courage

Diane Burd's Story

Diane Burd could be the mom next door. She was diagnosed with MS in 1978 at a time when very little was known about the disease. Since then, Diane has suffered from a variety of symptoms. First, she was statutorily blind for two years. She regained her eyesight, but was then paralyzed on her right side for another two years. Neurologists at the time had little recourse in fighting MS. They simply didn't know what to do to help her. No one did.

So in 1979, Diane stopped seeing the neurologists altogether and tried a support group. But when she got there, she wasn't prepared for what she found. There were wheelchairs. There were bent and twisted figures. There was pain. She wasn't ready for this. But there was nowhere left to go. It wasn't until 1993 that Diane started going back to see the neurologists. By then, medical strides had been made in the fight against MS: New treatments and medicines were available, a greater understanding was being achieved, and there was much Diane needed to catch up with.

Diane now lives with hope. Hope for a cure. Hope for a future. Hope for today. "You can't do anything about it, so you might as well smile," she says. Diane now believes that in life, people should take the word "try" out of their vocabulary. To try only leaves us open to failure.

Everyone in Diane's family knows about her illness, and they're all extremely supportive. Her husband, in particular, is a tremendous source of strength and encouragement. But it has been only recently that Diane has come to realize what a toll her illness has taken on him—the pain he shares with her, the frustration that eats away at him, the helplessness he lives with day after day.

Diane's son is now 26. She believes that her struggle with MS has made him a much more compassionate man, an understanding man, a good man. She always wished she could have had another child, but due to her MS, she was advised against it. But Diane doesn't complain, for not a moment goes by when she isn't eternally thankful for the undying love and support of her husband and son.

Richard Stoner's Story

Richard Stoner was 25 when he was first diagnosed with MS. He describes his first incident with MS as "flip-flopping around like a fish out of water." His doctor diagnosed him with the disease only two days before he was to join the Navy. Since the government offered treatments for MS,

Richard's doctor encouraged him to enlist. Richard's MS was in remission throughout his tour and stayed that way until he was 43. But by then, he had to have brain surgery to stop the pain from his trigeminal neuralgia, an illness that is sometimes associated with MS. The surgery stopped the pain, but it left his face deformed and numb. Not only that, but he was going through a divorce. An industrial engineer by trade, Richard began finding his work too stressful piled on top of everything else, and he soon retired.

Richard is in a wheelchair now and lives in New Jersey with his dog, Chelsea. No ordinary dog, Chelsea is a golden retriever who was trained for six months by the Dogs for Disabled before Richard worked with her for another week in South Carolina. After Chelsea came to live with Richard, a trainer continued working with them for another three months. Now, Chelsea helps Richard with tasks to make his life easier. Every morning, Chelsea brings Richard his phone so he can call the local police department's Reassurance Program (a program that services about 25 disabled people in the area) to let them know he's okay.

Richard loves drawing cartoons, particularly caricatures. He has drawn more than 24,000 cartoons at boardwalks, flea markets, and malls. He contributes a cartoon called "Chelsea . . . Service Dog" to a local newspaper geared toward people with disabilities. In addition, he is an active member of DATE—Disability Awareness Through Education, a group that travels to intermediate schools throughout New Jersey and talks to students about living and coping with disabilities. He is joined by someone who is hearing impaired, a quadriplegic, and an individual with cerebral palsy. Although Richard is disabled, he still drives locally. His car is rigged with hand controls and a platform lift that accommodates his wheelchair. Richard has quite a colorful use of language, a positive outlook on life, and an easygoing temperament. Everyone who knows him will agree that he's an absolute pleasure to be around.

Darian Kahl's and Samantha Ross's Story

Three years ago at the age of 25, Darian Kahl (on left) was diagnosed with MS. Her first bout with the disease occurred when she was still in college. It was there that Darian learned, as others have informed me, that many college medical services are not prepared to deal with illnesses that need more than a good dose of antibiotics. But since her diagnosis, Darian has learned to live with MS. She now teaches Special Education and works with autistic children. Her determination and love for her students propel her through each day—she has never missed a day of work.

Darian's choice is not to tell anyone at work about her diagnosis, but she shares her struggle with her friends and family. One of her hardest moments was when she had to tell her fiancé that she had MS. She remembers how difficult it was on the day they talked about her condition, their relationship, and their future. But the story has a happy ending! He is going to stick with her through thick and thin, he says, and they are currently planning their wedding!

Samantha Ross (pg. 62, right) is angry. When she was diagnosed with MS, she had just turned 20. It started out as a kidney infection that turned into a week-long hospital stay. The doctor heartlessly broke the news of her MS to her—over the phone! Slowly she hung up the phone, only to find that she was home alone, with no one to turn to. To make matters worse, she was soon to discover that there was no one her age she could talk to about MS. She tried support groups, but the members were much older than she was, many already in wheelchairs. So she reached out, seeking far and wide for the compassion and understanding of others her own age. She took out an ad, sending out the word for other young people with MS to come together, to meet and talk, to share and cope, and to offer arms to lean on and shoulders to cry on. This is how she met Darian.

Samantha's family has been very active in raising money for the MS cause. But Samantha is angry. She hasn't seen any results coming from all their hard work. In fact, when I told her why I was unhappy with a leading multiple sclerosis organization, she told me that her local chapter had recently remodeled their offices. That's why Samantha is angry. She wanted the money to go toward research—not new carpeting.

Joey McGauley's Story

Joey McGauley was diagnosed with MS when he was only 11 years old. Now at 16, he has had time to adapt, but in the beginning, it wasn't easy. Joey was the youngest person in the Philadelphia area to be diagnosed with MS. He had no one his age who could understand his pain and confusion, no one who could relate to what he was going through. His mom, Adele, said, "It really hit home when

Joey asked me if he was going to die from this. I told him, 'No, not _from_ it, _with_ it.'"

Shortly after Joey's diagnosis, several other youngsters in the area were diagnosed with MS. Joey started a support group for all of them. It was a bittersweet time, though. At last he could talk with others about his experience, but he also knew all too well the pain that the others were going through.

When I asked Joey how he dealt with MS, he said, matter-of-factly, "I just deal with it. I try to make it a regular day, a regular week. I go to school. Once I had to go to school with a patch over my eye."

Adele says that Joey does everything like other kids. "We've gone to Disneyland, he goes on rides, and he goes swimming."

Joey's medications were a big risk at the beginning because the treatments typically given to MS patients had never been tested on children. But all has worked out in the end, and his medications have become just another part of his daily routine. "We didn't change our lifestyle for the medicine," Adele explained. "If Joey's swimming and it's time for a shot, he comes out of the pool, gets his shot, and goes back in."

Adele feels that the hardest thing about the disease is the unpredictability. She used to enjoy making plans for the whole family—with Joey, his dad, and his older brother and sister. But the chaos of MS has taught her to live day by day.

All of Joey's friends know about his illness and are very supportive. When Joey is home resting due to an exacerbation of his symptoms, his friends all post get-well wishes on their Website, wishing him a speedy recovery. And every time Joey thinks of them, he can't help but smile.

Ebony Howard's Story

It was near the end of her sophomore year in college when Ebony was diagnosed with MS. Since her school wasn't equipped to diagnose her, she had to go to the only facility that could accommodate her—the psychiatric ward. She spent three days there while the doctors performed tests.

Ebony has always been accustomed to living with chronic illness, because her brother has diabetes. Since her mother died when she was still in high school, Ebony's MS has brought her closer to her dad. He is always active in donating to charities dedicated to the treatment of MS and diabetes, and he always has his ear out for new treatments on the market.

Ebony now lives at school with her roommates, and she studies English and acting. Her roommates play an integral part in keeping Ebony on track in her fight against MS— they make sure she takes her medicine, and they never let her forget that there are people who love and support her.

Ebony has become a writer, as well as the president of an acting group. She stays constantly active. With so much to do, she finds it hard to slow down and take it easy, even when she knows that's what's best for her.

Although Ebony doesn't dwell on being sick, she is constantly reminded of it. She finds the unpredictability of the disease infuriating. Nonetheless, her outlook on life is always positive and hopeful, especially now that she's determined not to let MS intrude into her busy schedule.

About the Author

Montel Williams is the Emmy Award-winning host of the nationally syndicated <u>Montel</u> show. As a highly decorated former Naval intelligence officer, motivational speaker, best-selling author, actor, and humanitarian, Williams is an example of personal achievement for people throughout the country. He is the proud father of four children.

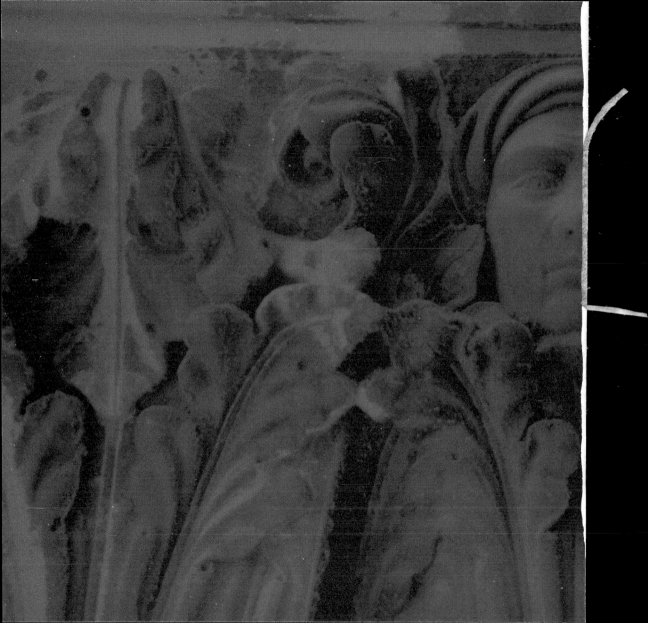